God Made Satan to Give Us Free Will to Choose

Apostle Bill Amor

God Made Satan to Give Us Free Will to Choose
written by Bill Amor
1st Edition © 2025 by Bill Amor
ISBN: 979-8-9995696-0-8

Scripture quotations taken from the Amplified® Bible, Copyright © 1954, 1958, 1962, 1964, 1965, 1987 by The Lockman Foundation. Used by permission. All rights reserved

CONTENTS

Contents

Synopsis of "God Made Satan to Give Us Free Will to Choose" by Apostle Bill Amor

Apostle Bill Amor's new book, *God Made Satan to Give Us Free Will to Choose*, delves into one of the most profound theological questions: why would an all-knowing, omnipotent God create Satan, knowing he would rebel? Amor explores this topic through the lens of free will, arguing that God's creation of Satan was integral to humanity's ability to make meaningful choices. The book emphasizes that without the presence of evil or opposition, true free will could not exist.

Amor examines biblical narratives such as the fall of Lucifer and Adam and Eve's disobedience in Eden, illustrating how these events highlight the importance of choice in God's divine plan. He asserts that God allowed for rebellion and temptation not out of malice but as a necessary component for love and obedience to be genuine. The book also reflects on how trials and temptations refine human character and deepen faith.

Through accessible language and scriptural references, Amor encourages readers to view challenges and moral dilemmas as opportunities to exercise their God-given freedom. Ultimately, he presents a hopeful message: while evil exists temporarily, God's greater plan ensures redemption and eternal good for those who choose Him.

This thought-provoking work invites believers and skeptics

alike to reconsider their understanding of free will, divine sovereignty, and the purpose behind life's struggles.

Scriptures suggest that the serpent, identified as Satan, was already fallen before the creation of man to provide humanity with the freedom to choose between good and evil. Key passages include:

1. **Ezekiel 28:12-17**: This passage describes a being in Eden who was created perfect but fell due to pride and corruption. Many interpret this as referring to Satan's fall before tempting Adam and Eve.[1]

2. **Isaiah 14:12-15**: This text speaks of a being (commonly associated with Lucifer/Satan) who sought to exalt himself above God but was cast down, indicating his rebellion occurred prior to human history.[2]

3. **Revelation 12:9**: It identifies Satan as "that ancient serpent" who deceives the world, linking him directly to the serpent in Genesis and confirming his fallen state before tempting humanity.[3]

4. **Genesis 3:1-5:** The serpent's craftiness and direct contradiction of God's word imply a pre-existing rebellion against God, consistent with Satan's role as a deceiver.[4]

These scriptures collectively support the theological view that Satan's fall preceded human creation, allowing for mankind's moral agency and ability to choose between good and evil.

The following scriptures from the Amplified Bible (AMP) provide evidence that the serpent, identified as Satan, was already fallen before the creation of man, allowing humanity to exercise free will and choose between good and evil. These passages are often interpreted by theologians to support this view.

1. Ezekiel 28:12-17 (AMP)

This passage is commonly understood as a dual prophecy, addressing both the King of Tyre and Satan's fall due to pride and rebellion.

"Son of man, take up a dirge (funeral poem to be sung) over the king of Tyre and say to him, 'Thus says the Lord God,
"You had the seal of perfection,
Full of wisdom and perfect in beauty.
You were in Eden, the garden of God;
Every precious stone was your covering:
The ruby, the topaz, and the diamond;
The beryl, the onyx, and the jasper;
The lapis lazuli, the turquoise, and the emerald;
And the gold, the workmanship of your settings and your sockets,
Was in you. They were prepared
On the day that you were created.
You were the anointed cherub who covers [and protects],
And I placed you there.
You were on the holy mountain of God;
You walked in the midst of the stones of fire [sparkling jewels].
You were blameless in your ways
From the day you were created

Until unrighteousness and evil were found in you. Through the abundance of your commerce
You were internally filled with lawlessness and violence, And you sinned; Therefore I have cast you out as a profane and unholy thing from the mountain of God. And I have destroyed you, O covering cherub, From the midst of the stones of fire. Your heart was proud and arrogant because of your beauty; You destroyed your wisdom for the sake of your splendor. I cast you to the ground; I lay you before kings That they might look at you."

This passage describes a being who was created perfect but fell due to pride—interpreted by many as referring to Satan's fall before he tempted Adam and Eve.

2. Isaiah 14:12-15 (AMP)

This text is often associated with Lucifer (Satan) seeking to exalt himself above God but being cast down.

"How you have fallen from heaven, O star of the morning [light-bringer], son of dawn! You have been cut down to the ground, You who have weakened the nations! But you said in your heart, 'I will ascend to heaven; I will raise my throne above the stars of God; I will sit on the mount of assembly In the remote parts of the north. I will ascend above the heights of clouds; I will make myself like The Most High.' But [in fact] you will be brought down to Sheol, To the remote recesses of the pit (the region of dead)."

This passage highlights Satan's ambition to usurp God's authority—a rebellion that led to his downfall prior to human history.

3. Revelation 12:9 (AMP)

Revelation explicitly identifies Satan as "the ancient serpent," linking him directly with Genesis 3.

"And [the great] dragon was thrown down—the age-old serpent who is called the devil and Satan, he who continually deceives and seduces the entire inhabited world; he was thrown down to earth, and his angels were thrown down with him."

This verse confirms that Satan had already fallen by Genesis 3 when he appeared as a deceiver in Eden.

4. Genesis 3:1-5 (AMP)

The serpent's actions in Eden demonstrate its pre-existing rebellion against God.

*"Now the serpent was more crafty (subtle, skilled in deceit) than any living creature of the field which the Lord God had made. And the serpent (Satan) said to the woman, 'Can it really be that God has said, "You shall not eat from any tree of *the garden"?'

The woman said to the serpent, 'We may eat fruit from the trees of the garden, except [the fruit] from the tree which is in the middle of the garden. God said,* "You shall not eat from it nor touch it," otherwise you will die.' But the serpent said to the woman, 'You certainly will not die! For God knows that on the day you eat from it your eyes will be opened [that is,* you will have greater awareness], and you will be like God,* knowing [the difference between] good and evil.'"**

Here we see Satan acting as a deceiver—contradicting God's word—which aligns with his role after his fall described elsewhere in Scripture.

Analysis

These passages collectively suggest that Satan's fall occurred before humanity's creation or shortly thereafter but prior to Adam's temptation in Eden. This timing allowed for mankind's moral agency—the ability for humans made "in God's image" (Genesis 1:27 AMP)—to freely choose between obedience or disobedience toward their Creator.

Theologically speaking:

1. Ezekiel 28 emphasizes Satan's original perfection followed by corruption.

2. Isaiah 14 portrays his prideful rebellion.

3. Revelation 12 links him directly with deception.

4. Genesis 3 shows him actively tempting humanity into sin.

Thus these scriptures together imply that Satan's fall preceded human history so that mankind could exercise free moral choice between good (obedience) or evil (disobedience).

1. The Concept of Free Will in Theology
This chapter explores the theological foundation of free will,

discussing its significance in Christian doctrine and how it allows humans to make moral choices. It references biblical texts like Moses 3:17 to explain the principle of agency.

2. The Creation of Satan: A Divine Purpose?
This chapter examines why God created Satan, analyzing scriptural interpretations that suggest Satan's role as a necessary opposition to good, enabling free will.

3. The Fall of Lucifer and Its Implications
Here, the narrative of Lucifer's rebellion is explored, focusing on his desire for power and its consequences (Isaiah 14:12–15). This chapter discusses how this event set the stage for humanity's moral testing.

4. Opposition in All Things: A Biblical Perspective
This chapter delves into the necessity of opposition for meaningful choice, citing biblical sources.

5. Adam and Eve's Choice in Eden
The story of Adam and Eve is analyzed as an archetype for human free will, emphasizing their decision to eat from the Tree of Knowledge as a pivotal moment in human history (Genesis 3).

6. The Role of Temptation in Free Will
This chapter discusses how temptation, often attributed to Satan, serves as a test for human morality and strengthens individual agency (James 1:13–15).

7. God's Sovereignty vs Human Freedom
A theological discussion on how God's omniscience coexists with human free will without predestining evil acts (Acts 4:27–28; Romans 8).

8. The Consequences of Choices: Good vs Evil
Explores how choices lead to natural consequences, both good and bad, referencing Galatians 6:7 and Revelation 22:12.

9. Redemption Through Christ's Sacrifice
Focuses on Jesus Christ's role in redeeming humanity from sin caused by misuse of free will, highlighting John 3:16 and Acts 4:27–28.

10. The Eschatological Restoration of Free Will
Analyzes the concept that in the eschaton (end times), humans will retain free will but be free from evil influences due to divine restoration (Revelation 21).

11. Misconceptions About Free Will and Predestination
Addresses common misunderstandings about predestination versus foreknowledge using examples like 1 Samuel 23:1-14.

12. Living with Free Will Today: Practical Applications
Concludes with practical advice on making righteous choices daily while resisting temptation through prayer and scripture study (Matthew 26:41).

Chapter 1: The Concept of Free Will in Theology

Free will is one of the most profound and debated concepts in theology, particularly within Christian doctrine. It refers to the ability of humans to make independent choices that are not coerced or predetermined by external forces, including divine intervention. This chapter explores the theological foundation of free will, its significance in Christian teachings, and how it enables humans to make moral decisions.

The Biblical Basis for Free Will

The concept of free will is deeply rooted in the Bible. From the very beginning, Scripture portrays humanity as endowed with the capacity to choose between obedience and disobedience, good and evil. One of the earliest examples comes from Genesis 2:16-17, where God commands Adam not to eat from the Tree of Knowledge of Good and Evil:

"And the Lord God commanded the man, saying, 'You may surely eat of every tree of the garden, but of the tree of the knowledge of good and evil you shall not eat, for in the day that you eat of it you shall surely die.'" (Genesis 2:16-17)

This command implies that Adam had a choice—he could obey God's directive or disobey it. The presence of this choice underscores a fundamental aspect of free will: without alternatives to choose from, there can be no true freedom.

Another key passage highlighting free will is found in Deuteronomy 30:19-20. Here, Moses addresses Israel before they enter the Promised Land:

"I call heaven and earth to witness against you today, that I have set before you life and death, blessing and curse. Therefore choose life, that you and your offspring may live." (Deuteronomy 30:19)

This verse explicitly presents a choice between two paths—life and death—and urges individuals to exercise their agency responsibly by choosing life.

Theological Significance

Free will holds immense theological significance because it underpins humanity's moral responsibility. If humans were incapable of making their own choices, they could neither be held accountable for their actions nor experience genuine love for God. Love requires freedom; coerced love is not love at all. This idea is echoed in Jesus' words in John 14:15:

"If you love me, you will keep my commandments." (John 14:15)

Here, Jesus emphasizes that obedience stems from love—a voluntary act rather than an obligation imposed by force.

Furthermore, free will allows humans to reflect God's image. According to Genesis 1:27:

"So God created man in his own image; in the image of God he created him; male and female he created them." (Genesis 1:27)

Being made in God's image includes possessing attributes such as rationality, creativity, and moral agency. Just as God exercises His sovereign will freely, humans are granted a measure of autonomy to make decisions within their finite existence.

Free Will and Moral Choices

The ability to choose between right and wrong lies at the heart of human existence. Without free will, morality would lose its meaning because actions would be predetermined rather than deliberate. For example:

- In Joshua 24:15, Joshua challenges Israel to decide whom they will serve: *"And if it is evil in your eyes to serve the Lord, choose this day whom you will serve... But as for me and my house, we will serve the Lord."* (Joshua 24:15)

This verse highlights personal accountability—the Israelites must consciously decide whether they will follow God or other gods.

- Similarly, Proverbs 3:5-6 encourages individuals to trust in God while acknowledging their role in decision-making: *"Trust in the Lord with all your heart; do not lean on your own understanding. In all your ways acknowledge him, and he will make straight your paths."*

These passages illustrate that while divine guidance is available through Scripture and prayer, individuals must actively choose whether or not to align themselves with God's principles.

Philosophical Perspectives on Free Will

In addition to biblical teachings, philosophical discussions have also shaped our understanding of free will within theology. Thinkers like Augustine grappled with reconciling human freedom with God's omniscience (the belief that God knows everything). Augustine argued that divine foreknowledge does not negate human freedom because knowing an action beforehand does not cause it to happen.

For instance:

- If a teacher knows a student well enough to predict they'll study hard for an exam but does nothing directly influencing their behavior during preparation—the student still acts freely despite being predictable.

Similarly:

- God's foreknowledge operates outside time constraints experienced by humans; He sees past/present/future simultaneously without interfering directly unless necessary according-to-His-purpose-plan-for-good Romans 8:28).

The Concept of Free Will in Theology

- This chapter explores the theological foundation of free will, discussing its significance in Christian doctrine and how it allows humans to make moral choices. Free will is a cornerstone of many Christian teachings, emphasizing that God created humanity with the ability to choose between good and evil. This capacity for choice is what distinguishes humans from other creations and reflects the image of God within them (Genesis 1:26-27).

- The Bible frequently underscores the importance of free will in shaping human destiny. For instance, Deuteronomy 30:19 states, "I have set before you life and death, blessings and curses. Now choose life, so that you and your children may live." This verse highlights the divine invitation to exercise free will responsibly by choosing paths aligned with God's commandments.

- Free will also plays a critical role in understanding the nature of love and obedience in Christian theology. Love, as described in 1 Corinthians 13, must be freely given to hold true value. If humans were compelled to love or obey God without choice, their actions would lack authenticity. Thus, free will is essential for genuine relationships between humanity and God.

• Challenges & Misconceptions About Free Will

- Despite its foundational role in theology, the concept of free will has been subject to various challenges and misconceptions throughout history. One common misunderstanding involves reconciling God's omniscience with human freedom. Critics often ask: If God knows everything—including future events—how can humans truly have free will? This question has led to extensive theological debate.

- Christian thinkers like Augustine and Thomas Aquinas have addressed this issue by distinguishing between God's foreknowledge and predestination. They argue that while God knows what choices individuals will make, His knowledge does not cause those choices. In this view, divine foreknowledge exists outside time as humans experience it; thus, God's awareness of future events does not negate human agency.

- Another challenge arises from interpretations of predestination found in passages like Romans 8:29-30 and Ephesians 1:4-5. Some argue these verses suggest that God preordains certain individuals for salvation or condemnation, seemingly undermining free will. However, many theologians interpret these passages as emphasizing God's overarching plan for redemption rather than negating individual choice. They assert that predestination refers to God's desire for all people to be saved (1 Timothy 2:4), leaving room for personal decision-making.

- Additionally, some skeptics question whether external influences—such as societal pressures or biological predispositions—limit true freedom of choice. While it is undeniable that external factors shape human be-havior to some extent, Christian theology maintains that individuals retain ultimate responsibility for their actions (Ezekiel 18:20). The presence of external influences does not eliminate moral accountability but instead highlights the complexity of exercising free will in a fallen world.

- Finally, there is often confusion about the relationship between grace and free will in salvation. Some tradi-tions emphasize human effort in achieving righteous-ness (synergism), while others stress reliance on di-vine grace alone (monergism). The balance between these perspectives varies among denominations but generally acknowledges both God's initiative in offering grace and humanity's response through faith (Ephesians 2:8-9).

- By addressing these challenges and misconceptions, this chapter aims to provide a clearer understanding of free will's theological significance. It emphasizes that while questions remain about its precise mechanics, free will remains central to Christian teachings on morality, love, and salvation.

The concept of predestination and the idea that God hardens hearts are deeply rooted in theological discussions, particularly within Christian traditions. These ideas often raise questions about the coexistence of divine sovereignty and human free will. To understand these concepts, it is essential to examine their biblical foundation and theological implications.

- The notion that God hardens hearts is explicitly mentioned in several passages of the Bible, most notably in the story of Pharaoh during the Exodus. In Exodus 9:12, it states, "But the Lord hardened Pharaoh's heart, and he would not listen to Moses and Aaron, just as the Lord had said to Moses." This act of hardening Pharaoh's heart was part of God's plan to demonstrate His power and glory through the plagues and ultimately deliver Israel from slavery. Similarly, Romans 9:18 reinforces this idea: "Therefore God has mercy on whom he wants to have mercy, and he hardens whom he wants to harden." These verses suggest that God's intervention in human decisions serves a greater purpose within His divine plan.

- Predestination is another significant theological concept that emphasizes God's ultimate control over all events and outcomes. Ephesians 1:4-5 states, "For He chose us in Him before the creation of the world to be holy and blameless in His sight. In love He predestined us for adoption to sonship through Jesus Christ, in accordance with His pleasure and will." This passage highlights that God's plan for humanity was established before creation itself. Similarly, Romans 8:29-30 explains that those whom God foreknew were predestined to be conformed to the image of His Son.

- These doctrines can appear paradoxical when juxtaposed with human free will. However, many theologians argue that God's sovereignty does not negate human responsibility but rather works alongside it in ways beyond human comprehension. For instance, while Judas Iscariot's betrayal of Jesus was foretold (John 13:21-27), Judas still acted out of his own volition. This interplay between divine foreordination and human choice underscores a complex relationship where both coexist without contradiction from a theological perspective.

- The hardening of hearts and predestination serve as reminders of God's omnipotence and omniscience. They illustrate that all events unfold according to His divine will, even when they involve human actions or decisions. While these concepts may challenge our understanding of justice or fairness, they ultimately point toward a greater purpose—God's plan for redemption and His desire for humanity to recognize His sovereignty.

- In conclusion, the doctrines of God hardening hearts and predestination emphasize that everything occurs within the framework of God's eternal plan. They affirm His absolute authority over creation while inviting believers to trust in His wisdom and purpose. Although these ideas may seem difficult to reconcile with our limited understanding, they encourage faith in a God who orchestrates all things for His glory and the ultimate good of those who love Him (Romans 8:28).

Conclusion for Chapter 1: The Concept of Free Will in Theology

- In conclusion, the concept of free will is a cornerstone of Christian theology, emphasizing humanity's unique ability to make moral choices. Rooted in the belief that God created humans in His image (Genesis 1:27), free will underscores the divine intention for individuals to act as moral agents, capable of choosing between good and evil. This capacity for choice is what distinguishes humanity from other creations and reflects God's desire for a genuine relationship with His people—one based on love and voluntary obedience rather than coercion.

- The biblical narrative consistently highlights the importance of free will, from Adam and Eve's decision in the Garden of Eden (Genesis 3) to the exhortations found throughout scripture encouraging believers to choose righteousness over sin (Deuteronomy 30:19). These examples illustrate that while God provides guidance through His commandments and teachings, He does not impose His will upon humanity. Instead, He allows individuals to navigate their own paths, even when those choices lead to consequences that align with or deviate from His divine plan.

- Free will also serves as a foundation for understanding human accountability. Scriptures such as Galatians 6:7 ("Do not be deceived: God cannot be mocked. A man reaps what he sows.") affirm that our choices have real consequences, both temporal and eternal. This principle reinforces the idea that moral agency is not only a gift but also a responsibility entrusted to each person.

- Ultimately, free will is integral to the Christian understanding of salvation and redemption. It enables individuals to respond freely to God's grace through faith in Jesus Christ (Ephesians 2:8-9), making salvation a personal decision rather than an imposed outcome. By granting humanity free will, God demonstrates His respect for human autonomy while inviting all people into a loving relationship with Him—a relationship defined by choice rather than compulsion.

Chapter 2: The Creation of Satan: A Divine Purpose?

The question of why God created Satan is one that has per-
plexed theologians, scholars, and believers for centuries. In
Christian theology, Satan is often portrayed as the ultimate
adversary, a being who opposes God and tempts humanity
into sin. However, when viewed through the lens of free will,
some interpretations suggest that Satan's existence serves
a divine purpose—namely, to provide the necessary opposition that enables humans to exercise their free will. This
chapter delves into scriptural interpretations and theological
reasoning to explore this idea.

The Nature of Free Will in Christian Theology

Free will is a cornerstone of Christian theology. It is the ability to choose between good and evil, right and wrong, obedience and disobedience. Without free will, human beings
would be mere automatons, incapable of genuine love or
moral responsibility. For free will to exist meaningfully, there
must be real choices available—choices that carry consequences.

In this context, the existence of Satan can be seen as
integral to the concept of free will. If there were no opposition to God's goodness—no alternative path—then humans
would not truly have the freedom to choose. As C.S. Lewis
famously wrote in _Mere Christianity_, "Free will... though it
makes evil possible, is also the only thing that makes possible any love or goodness or joy worth having."[1]

Scriptural Accounts of Satan's Creation

The Bible provides several passages that shed light on Satan's origins and his role in God's creation. One key text often cited is Isaiah 14:12-15, which describes the fall of a figure referred to as "Lucifer," traditionally interpreted as Satan:

"How you have fallen from heaven, morning star, son of the dawn! You have been cast down to the earth, you who once laid low the nations! You said in your heart, 'I will ascend to the heavens; I will raise my throne above the stars of God; I will sit enthroned on the mount of assembly, on the utmost heights of Mount Zaphon. I will ascend above the tops of the clouds; I will make myself like the Most High.' But you are brought down to the realm of the dead, to the depths of the pit." (Isaiah 14:12-15 NIV)

This passage portrays Lucifer as a being created with great beauty and power but who fell from grace due to pride and rebellion against God. Ezekiel 28:12-17 offers a similar narrative:

"You were anointed as a guardian cherub, for so I ordained you. You were on the holy mount of God; you walked among the fiery stones. You were blameless in your ways from the day you were created till wickedness was found in you." (Ezekiel 28:14-15 NIV)

These verses suggest that Satan was originally created

good but chose rebellion against God out of pride and ambition. His fall illustrates not only his misuse of free will but also sets up his role as an adversary—a necessary counterpoint for human moral testing.

Opposition as Necessary for Free Will

One central theme in Christian theology is that opposition is essential for meaningful choice. Without alternatives—without something or someone opposing God's goodness—there would be no real decision-making process for humanity.

James 1:13-15 explains how temptation works within this framework:

"When tempted, no one should say, 'God is tempting me.' For God cannot be tempted by evil, nor does he tempt anyone; but each person is tempted when they are dragged away by their own evil desire and enticed. Then, after desire has conceived, it gives birth to sin; and sin, when it is full-grown, gives birth to death." (James 1:13-15 NIV)

While God does not directly tempt anyone toward sin (as James clarifies), He allows temptation—and by extension Satan—to exist so that humans can exercise their agency. Temptation acts as a test or proving ground for moral character.

Satan's role as "the tempter" is explicitly mentioned in Matthew 4:1-11 during Jesus' time in the wilderness:

"Then Jesus was led by the Spirit into the wilderness to be tempted by the devil... The tempter came to him and said..." (Matthew 4:1-3 NIV)

Here we see Satan fulfilling his role as an oppositional force even against Christ Himself. This encounter underscores how opposition sharpens resolve and strengthens faith.

Why Would an All-Good God Allow Evil?

A common objection raised against this interpretation is why an all-good God would create a being like Satan if He knew he would rebel and bring evil into creation. The answer lies in understanding God's ultimate purpose for humanity.

God's creation was designed with love at its core (1 John 4:8). Love requires freedom—it cannot be coerced or programmed. By creating beings with free will—including angels like Lucifer—God allowed for both obedience born out of love and rebellion born out of pride.

Romans 8:28 offers reassurance about God's sovereignty over even seemingly negative events:

"And we know that in all things God works for the good of those who love him, who have been called according to his purpose." (Romans 8:28 NIV)

Even though Satan's rebellion introduced suffering into creation, it also set up conditions under which humans could freely choose loyalty to God over selfishness or sin.

Conclusion

From a theological perspective, Satan's existence serves a divine purpose by providing necessary opposition within God's plan for humanity's moral development. His role as tempter ensures that humans face real choices between good and evil—a prerequisite for genuine free will.

While difficult questions remain about why God permits suffering caused by evil forces like Satan, many theologians argue that such challenges ultimately lead individuals closer to understanding their dependence on divine grace.

In summary, while it may seem paradoxical at first glance that an all-good God would create a being like Satan who opposes Him so vehemently, this act aligns with His over-arching goal: enabling humanity's capacity for meaningful choice rooted in love rather than compulsion.

Chapter 3: The Fall of Lucifer and Its Implications

The story of Lucifer's fall is one of the most significant narratives in Christian theology, as it provides a framework for understanding the existence of evil, the role of free will, and the moral testing of humanity. This chapter delves into the biblical account of Lucifer's rebellion, his desire for power, and the consequences that followed. It also explores how this event set the stage for humanity's ongoing struggle between good and evil.

The Origin of Lucifer

Lucifer, whose name means "light-bearer" or "morning star," is traditionally understood to have been a high-ranking angel created by God. He was described as being perfect in beauty and wisdom, adorned with splendor (Ezekiel 28:12-15). While Ezekiel 28 primarily addresses the King of Tyre, many theologians interpret parts of this passage as an allegorical reference to Lucifer due to its description of a being who was in Eden and who fell from perfection.

Isaiah 14:12-15 further elaborates on Lucifer's fall:

"How you have fallen from heaven, morning star, son of the dawn! You have been cast down to the earth, you who once laid low the nations! You said in your heart, 'I will ascend to the heavens; I will raise my throne above the stars of God; I will sit enthroned on the mount of assembly... I will make myself like the Most High.' But you are brought down to the

realm of the dead, to the depths of the pit." (NIV)

This passage portrays Lucifer as a being consumed by pride and ambition. His desire was not merely to serve God but to usurp God's authority and elevate himself above all creation. This act of rebellion marked his transition from a glorious angelic being into Satan—the adversary.

The Nature of Lucifer's Rebellion

Lucifer's rebellion was rooted in pride and self-exaltation. According to Christian theology, God endowed angels with free will just as He did humans. This freedom allowed them to choose obedience or disobedience. Lucifer chose disobedience by aspiring to be equal with God—a direct violation of his created purpose.

Theologians often emphasize that this rebellion was not simply an isolated act but a deliberate rejection of God's sovereignty. By attempting to "make himself like the Most High," Lucifer sought autonomy apart from God's rule. This act introduced sin into creation for the first time.

The Consequences for Lucifer

As a result of his rebellion, Lucifer was cast out of heaven along with other angels who followed him (Revelation 12:7-9). These fallen angels became demons—spiritual beings opposed to God's purposes. Revelation describes this cosmic battle:

"Then war broke out in heaven. Michael and his angels fought against the dragon, and the dragon and his angels fought back. But he was not strong enough, and they lost their place in heaven. The great dragon was hurled down— that ancient serpent called the devil or Satan, who leads the whole world astray." (Revelation 12:7-9)

This expulsion marked Satan's transition from an exalted position in heaven to becoming an adversary on Earth.

Implications for Humanity

The fall of Lucifer had profound implications for humanity because it introduced opposition into God's creation. Satan became synonymous with temptation and deception—actively working against God's plan for humankind.

1. **Temptation in Eden**
   One immediate consequence was Satan's role in tempting Adam and Eve in Genesis 3. Disguised as a serpent, he deceived them into eating from the Tree of Knowledge by questioning God's commandment ("Did God really say...?") and appealing to their desire for wisdom ("You will be like God"). This act led to humanity's fall into sin—a direct result of succumbing to Satan's influence.

2. **Moral Testing**

With Satan's presence came moral testing for humanity. His role as tempter ensures that humans must actively choose between obedience to God or yielding to sinful desires (James 1:13-15). Without opposition or alternatives presented by Satan, free will would lack meaningful exercise since there would be no real choice involved.

3. **Spiritual Warfare**
   The Bible frequently describes life on Earth as a spiritual battlefield where believers must resist Satan's schemes (Ephesians 6:11-12). Christians are called upon to stand firm against temptation through faith in Christ while recognizing that their struggle is not merely against flesh but against spiritual forces aligned with Satan.

4. **God's Sovereignty Amidst Evil**
   Despite Satan's rebellion and continued opposition, Christian theology asserts that God remains sovereign over all creation—including Satan himself (Job 1:6-12). In allowing Satan limited freedom within His divine plan, God provides humans with opportunities for growth through trials while ultimately ensuring that good triumphs over evil (Romans 8:28).

Conclusion

The fall of Lucifer serves as both a cautionary tale about pride and disobedience and an explanation for why evil exists within creation despite being made by a good God. It underscores themes central to Christian theology: free will, moral responsibility, redemption through Christ's sacrifice (John 3:16), and ultimate victory over sin at history's culmination (Revelation 20:10).

By understanding this narrative within its biblical context—not merely as myth but as theological truth—believers can better grasp their own role within God's redemptive plan while navigating life's moral challenges underpinned by free will.

Chapter 4: Opposition in All Things: A Biblical Perspective

The concept of opposition is deeply embedded in the fabric of Christian theology and is essential for understanding the role of free will in human existence. Without opposition, the ability to make meaningful choices would be rendered moot. This chapter explores the necessity of opposition as presented in biblical scripture, emphasizing its role in allowing individuals to exercise their free will and grow spiritually.

The Necessity of Opposition for Free Will

Opposition is a fundamental principle that allows humans to distinguish between good and evil, light and darkness, truth and falsehood. Without contrasting forces, there would be no context within which moral decisions could be made. This idea is rooted in the very nature of creation as described in Genesis. In Genesis 1:3-4, God creates light and separates it from darkness, establishing a duality that symbolizes the broader concept of opposition throughout scripture:

"And God said, 'Let there be light,' and there was light. God saw that the light was good, and He separated the light from the darkness." (Genesis 1:3-4)

This act of separation sets a precedent for understanding how opposites are necessary for defining one another. Light has meaning because darkness exists; similarly, good can only be understood in contrast to evil.

The Role of Opposition in Moral Growth

The presence of opposition also serves as a catalyst for moral growth. James 1:2-4 highlights how trials and challenges—forms of opposition—are instrumental in developing perseverance and maturity:

"Consider it pure joy, my brothers and sisters, whenever you face trials of many kinds, because you know that the testing of your faith produces perseverance. Let perseverance finish its work so that you may be mature and complete, not lacking anything." (James 1:2-4)

Here, James underscores that facing difficulties is not merely an unfortunate aspect of life but a necessary process through which individuals grow stronger in their faith and character.

Similarly, Romans 5:3-5 reinforces this idea by linking suffering (a form of opposition) to hope:

"Not only so, but we also glory in our sufferings, because we know that suffering produces perseverance; perseverance, character; and character, hope." (Romans 5:3-5)

These passages suggest that without challenges or opposing forces to overcome, humans would lack opportunities for spiritual refinement.

Good vs Evil: A Biblical Dichotomy

The Bible frequently presents life as a battleground between good and evil—a dichotomy that underscores the importance of choice. In Deuteronomy 30:19-20, Moses calls upon Israel to choose between life and death:

"This day I call the heavens and the earth as witnesses against you that I have set before you life and death, blessings and curses. Now choose life so that you and your children may live." (Deuteronomy 30:19)

This passage illustrates how God provides humanity with clear options but leaves it up to individuals to decide their path. The existence of both blessings (good) and curses (evil) ensures that choices carry weight.

Another example comes from Proverbs 4:18-19:

"The path of the righteous is like the morning sun, shining ever brighter till the full light of day. But the way of the wicked is like deep darkness; they do not know what makes them stumble." (Proverbs 4:18-19)

Here again is a stark contrast between righteousness (light) and wickedness (darkness), reinforcing how opposition defines moral pathways.

Satan's Role as an Opponent

In Christian theology, Satan often embodies opposition by tempting humans away from righteousness. His role as "the adversary" highlights how his actions create opportunities for humans to exercise their free will by resisting temptation.

In Matthew 4:1-11, Jesus Himself faces direct temptation from Satan during His time in the wilderness. Each temptation represents an opportunity for Jesus to choose obedience over sin:

"Then Jesus was led by the Spirit into the wilderness to be tempted by the devil... Jesus said to him [Satan], 'Away from me! For it is written: Worship the Lord your God, and serve Him only.' Then the devil left Him." (Matthew 4:1-11)

This account demonstrates how even Christ faced opposition but used it as an opportunity to affirm His commitment to God's will.

The Balance Between Justice and Mercy

Opposition also plays a critical role in balancing justice with mercy—two attributes central to God's nature. Psalm 89:14 describes this balance:

"Righteousness and justice are the foundation of Your throne; love and faithfulness go before You." (Psalm 89:14)

Justice requires accountability for wrongdoing (opposition against sin), while mercy offers forgiveness through repentance. Together they create a dynamic tension that allows humans to experience both consequences for their actions and redemption through grace.

Conclusion

Opposition is not merely an incidental aspect of human existence but a divinely ordained mechanism through which free will operates meaningfully. By presenting humanity with choices between good and evil—and allowing them to face trials—God provides opportunities for growth, learning, and spiritual development.

Without opposition:

- There would be no context for moral decision-making.

- Trials would not refine character or strengthen faith.

- The concepts of justice or mercy would lose significance.

As such, opposition remains integral not only to individual lives but also to God's overarching plan for humanity's salvation.

Chapter 5: Adam and Eve's Choice in Eden

The story of Adam and Eve, as presented in the Book of Genesis, is one of the most well-known narratives in religious history. It serves as a foundational account for understanding human free will within Judeo-Christian theology. This chapter examines their decision to eat from the Tree of Knowledge of Good and Evil, analyzing it as an archetype for human free will and moral responsibility.

The Setting: The Garden of Eden

The narrative begins with God creating a perfect world, including the Garden of Eden, where Adam and Eve were placed to live (Genesis 2:8-15). In this paradise, they were given everything they needed to thrive—abundant food, companionship, and direct communion with God. However, there was one specific commandment given to them: they were not to eat from the Tree of Knowledge of Good and Evil. As stated in Genesis 2:16-17:

"And the Lord God commanded the man, saying, 'Of every tree of the garden thou mayest freely eat; but of the tree of the knowledge of good and evil, thou shalt not eat of it: for in the day that thou eatest thereof thou shalt surely die.'"

This prohibition established a clear boundary and introduced a choice. It is important to note that without this commandment—and without the presence of an alternative action (eating from the forbidden tree)—there would have been no opportunity for Adam and Eve to exercise free will.

The Role of Free Will

Free will is central to this story because it highlights humanity's ability to make decisions independently. By placing the Tree of Knowledge in Eden and forbidding its fruit, God created a scenario where obedience or disobedience was possible. Without such a choice, Adam and Eve would have been mere automatons—creatures incapable of moral reasoning or personal growth.

The inclusion of free will also underscores God's desire for genuine love and obedience from humanity. Love that is coerced or forced is not true love; similarly, obedience without choice lacks meaning. By giving Adam and Eve free will, God allowed them to choose whether they would trust Him and follow His command.

The Temptation by the Serpent

In Genesis 3:1-5, we are introduced to another key figure in this narrative—the serpent. Described as "more subtle than any beast of the field," the serpent tempts Eve by questioning God's command:

"Yea, hath God said, Ye shall not eat of every tree of the garden?" (Genesis 3:1)

This question introduces doubt into Eve's mind about God's intentions. The serpent goes further by directly contradicting God's warning:

"Ye shall not surely die: For God doth know that in the day ye eat thereof, then your eyes shall be opened, and ye shall be as gods, knowing good and evil." (Genesis 3:4-5)

Here we see an appeal to pride and curiosity—two powerful motivators that often influence human decision-making. The serpent suggests that God is withholding something valuable from Adam and Eve: knowledge that would elevate them to divine status.

The Decision

Faced with this temptation, Eve evaluates her options. Genesis 3:6 describes her thought process:

"And when the woman saw that the tree was good for food, and that it was pleasant to the eyes, and a tree to be desired to make one wise, she took of the fruit thereof, and did eat; and gave also unto her husband with her; and he did eat."

Eve's decision reflects three key factors:

1. **Physical Desire** – She saw that «the tree was good for food.»

2. **Aesthetic Appeal** – It was «pleasant to the eyes.»

3. **Intellectual Aspiration** – It was «a tree to be desired to make one wise.»

These motivations illustrate how complex human choices can be—often influenced by physical needs, emotional responses, and intellectual curiosity.

Adam's subsequent choice to partake in the fruit demonstrates his own exercise of free will. While some interpretations suggest he ate out of solidarity with Eve or fear of being alone again (as she was created as his companion), his action nonetheless represents an independent decision.

The Consequences

The immediate consequence of their disobedience was a newfound awareness:

"And the eyes of them both were opened, and they knew that they were naked; and they sewed fig leaves together, and made themselves aprons." (Genesis 3:7)

This newfound knowledge brought shame—a stark contrast to their previous state of innocence (Genesis 2:25). Their relationship with God also changed dramatically; when He came looking for them in the garden (Genesis 3:8-10), they hid out of fear rather than approaching Him openly.

God's response included several punishments:

- For Eve: Increased pain in childbirth and subordination within her relationship with Adam (Genesis 3:16).

- For Adam: Hard labor required to produce food from a cursed ground (Genesis 3:17-19).

- For both: Expulsion from Eden (Genesis 3:23-24).

These consequences highlight an essential principle about free will—it comes with responsibility. Choices have repercussions that cannot always be undone.

A Pivotal Moment in Human History

The decision made by Adam and Eve has been interpreted as a pivotal moment not only within biblical history but also within theological discussions about human nature. Their choice introduced sin into the world—a concept often referred to as "the Fall." This event explains why humans experience suffering, death, and separation from God.

However, it also set into motion God's plan for redemption through Jesus Christ—a theme explored later in Scripture (Romans 5:12-21). In this sense, their exercise of free will ultimately led to both humanity's greatest tragedy (the Fall) and its greatest hope (salvation).

Conclusion

The story of Adam and Eve serves as an archetype for human free will because it encapsulates key elements:

1. A clear commandment establishing moral boundaries.

2. An external temptation challenging those boundaries.

3. A conscious decision made by individuals weighing various factors.

4. Consequences resulting from those decisions.

Through this narrative, we see how free will allows humans not only to make choices but also to grow spiritually by learning from their mistakes—a process central to Christian theology.

Chapter 6: The Role of Temptation in Free Will

Temptation is an integral part of the human experience and plays a significant role in the exercise of free will. In theological discussions, temptation is often seen as a mechanism through which individuals are tested, allowing them to demonstrate their moral character and make choices that align with or deviate from divine principles. This chapter explores the nature of temptation, its connection to free will, and how it serves as a critical component in the development of human morality.

The Nature of Temptation

Temptation can be broadly defined as an enticement or urge to engage in behavior that is contrary to moral or ethical standards. From a Christian perspective, temptation is frequently associated with Satan, who is portrayed in scripture as the adversary seeking to lead humanity away from God's will. For example, in the New Testament, Satan tempts Jesus in the wilderness by offering Him power and material wealth if He would abandon His divine mission (Matthew 4:1–11). This narrative illustrates how temptation often appeals to human desires but ultimately challenges individuals to choose between self-interest and obedience to God.

It is important to note that while Satan may be depicted as the source of temptation, scripture emphasizes that God does not tempt anyone. James 1:13–15 states: "When tempted, no one should say, 'God is tempting me.' For God cannot be tempted by evil, nor does he tempt anyone; but each person is tempted when they are dragged away by their own evil desire and enticed. Then, after desire has conceived, it gives birth to sin; and sin, when it is full-grown, gives birth to death." This passage highlights that temptation arises from internal desires rather than being imposed directly by God.

Temptation as a Test of Morality

The presence of temptation serves a dual purpose: it reveals human vulnerabilities while also providing opportunities for growth. By resisting temptation, individuals strengthen their moral resolve and demonstrate their commitment to virtuous living. Conversely, succumbing to temptation can lead to spiritual consequences such as guilt, separation from God, and harm to oneself or others.

The story of Adam and Eve in Genesis 3 exemplifies this dynamic. When tempted by the serpent (often interpreted as Satan), Eve chooses to eat from the Tree of Knowledge of Good and Evil despite God's explicit command not to do so. This act introduces sin into the world but also underscores humanity's capacity for choice—a fundamental aspect of free will. While Adam and Eve's decision had profound consequences for themselves and their descendants, it also set the stage for redemption through Christ.

Strengthening Free Will Through Resistance

Resisting temptation requires conscious effort and reliance

on spiritual resources such as prayer, scripture study, and community support. Jesus' response during His wilderness trial provides a model for overcoming temptation: He counters each of Satan's offers with scriptural truths (Matthew 4:4–10). This approach demonstrates how knowledge of God's word can empower individuals to make righteous choices even under pressure.

Furthermore, enduring trials can lead to personal growth and deeper faith. Romans 5:3–5 states: "Not only so, but we also glory in our sufferings because we know that suffering produces perseverance; perseverance, character; and character, hope." While this passage primarily addresses broader forms of suffering rather than specific temptations, it underscores the transformative potential inherent in facing challenges.

The Role of Grace

While humans are called upon to resist temptation actively using their free will, Christian theology teaches that divine grace plays an essential role in this process. According to 1 Corinthians 10:13: "No temptation has overtaken you except what is common to mankind. And God is faithful; he will not let you be tempted beyond what you can bear. But when you are tempted he will also provide a way out so that you can endure it." This assurance reminds believers that they are never alone in their struggles against sin—God provides strength and guidance for those who seek His help.

Conclusion

Temptation serves as both a challenge and an opportunity within the framework of free will. It tests human morality by presenting choices between good and evil while offering chances for spiritual growth through resistance. By relying on divine grace alongside personal effort—through prayerful reflection on scripture—individuals can navigate life's trials successfully while strengthening their relationship with God.

Chapter 7: God's Sovereignty vs Human Freedom

The relationship between God's sovereignty and human freedom has been a central topic in Christian theology for centuries. This chapter explores how the omniscience and omnipotence of God coexist with the concept of free will, particularly focusing on how God does not predestine evil acts but allows humans to make their own moral choices. By examining key biblical passages and theological interpretations, we can better understand this complex interplay.

Understanding God's Sovereignty

God's sovereignty refers to His supreme authority and power over all creation. Scripture consistently affirms that God is in control of the universe, orchestrating events according to His divine plan. For example, Psalm 103:19 states, "The Lord has established his throne in heaven, and his kingdom rules over all." Similarly, Isaiah 46:9–10 declares, "I am God, and there is no other; I am God, and there is none like me. I make known the end from the beginning, from ancient times, what is still to come. I say, 'My purpose will stand, and I will do all that I please.'"

These verses emphasize God's omniscience (His ability to know everything) and omnipotence (His unlimited power). However, this raises an important question: If God knows everything that will happen and has the power to intervene in any situation, how can humans truly have free will? Does this mean that our actions are predetermined?

The Nature of Free Will

Free will is the ability to make choices that are not coerced or predetermined by external forces. In Christian theology, free will is essential for moral responsibility. Without it, humans could not be held accountable for their actions—good or evil.

The Bible affirms human free will in numerous passages. For instance:

- **Deuteronomy 30:19**: "This day I call the heavens and the earth as witnesses against you that I have set before you life and death, blessings and curses. Now choose life so that you and your children may live."

- **Joshua 24:15:** "But if serving the Lord seems undesirable to you, then choose for yourselves this day whom you will serve."

These verses highlight that humans are given real choices with real consequences. The ability to choose between good and evil is foundational to our relationship with God.

Reconciling Sovereignty with Free Will

At first glance, God's sovereignty might seem incompatible with human free will. If God knows everything in advance (foreknowledge), does this mean He causes everything to happen? The answer lies in understanding the distinction between foreknowledge and predestination.

Foreknowledge vs Predestination

Foreknowledge refers to God's ability to know what will happen before it occurs. Predestination implies that God determines every event beforehand. While some theological traditions (such as Calvinism) emphasize predestination more heavily than others (like Arminianism), many theologians argue that foreknowledge does not necessitate causation.

For example:

- **Acts 4:27–28** describes how Herod, Pontius Pilate, the Gentiles, and the people of Israel conspired against Jesus Christ. The passage states that they did «what your power and will had decided beforehand should happen.» This demonstrates that while God foreknew these events as part of His redemptive plan through Christ›s crucifixion, those involved acted out of their own volition.

- **Romans 8:29–30** speaks of those whom God «foreknew» being «predestined» to be conformed to the image of His Son. Here again, foreknowledge precedes predestination; it does not negate human choice but rather works alongside it within God's overarching plan.

In other words:

1. **God's foreknowledge allows Him to see all possible outcomes without forcing any particular one upon individuals.**

2. **Human beings retain genuine freedom to make choices within the framework of God's sovereign plan.**

Permitting Evil Without Causing It

A key aspect of reconciling sovereignty with free will involves understanding how God permits evil without being its author. The Bible teaches that while God allows evil acts for a time (due to human sinfulness), He does not cause them or delight in them:

- **James 1:13:** "When tempted, no one should say, 'God is tempting me.' For God cannot be tempted by evil, nor does he tempt anyone."

- **Habakkuk 1:13**: "Your eyes are too pure to look on evil; you cannot tolerate wrongdoing."

Instead of causing evil directly:

1. **God permits human beings to exercise their free will,** even when it leads to sinful actions.

2. **God can bring good out of evil situations,** demonstrating His ultimate sovereignty over even the worst circumstances (Genesis 50:20; Romans 8:28).

For example:

- Joseph's brothers sold him into slavery out of jealousy (Genesis 37). While their actions were sinful, God used this situation for good by elevating Joseph to a position where he could save many lives during a famine.

- The crucifixion of Jesus was an act of profound injustice carried out by sinful men; yet it became the means through which salvation was made available to humanity.

Practical Implications

Understanding how God's sovereignty coexists with human freedom has several practical implications for believers:

1. **Trust in God's Plan**: Even when faced with suffering or injustice caused by human sinfulness or natural disasters beyond our control, we can trust that God's ultimate purposes are good (Jeremiah 29:11).

2. **Moral Responsibility**: Recognizing our freedom means accepting responsibility for our choices—both good and bad—and striving daily toward righteousness.

3. **Hope Amidst Evil:** Knowing that God can redeem even the darkest situations gives us hope amidst trials.

Conclusion

The coexistence of God's sovereignty with human freedom remains a profound mystery but one deeply rooted in Scripture. By distinguishing between foreknowledge and causation—and recognizing how divine providence works alongside human agency—we gain a clearer understanding of this theological tension.

Ultimately:

- **God's sovereignty ensures His plans cannot be thwarted (Job 42:2).**

- **Human free will ensures we are active participants in those plans—not mere puppets but beloved children invited into relationship with our Creator (John 15:15).**

Chapter 8: The Consequences of Choices: Good vs Evil

The concept of free will is deeply intertwined with the idea of consequences. Every choice we make, whether good or evil, carries with it a set of natural outcomes. This chapter explores how human decisions lead to consequences that shape not only individual lives but also the broader moral fabric of society. By examining biblical teachings and theological perspectives, we can better understand the relationship between free will, moral responsibility, and divine justice.

The Principle of Sowing and Reaping

One of the clearest biblical explanations of the connection between choices and their consequences is found in Galatians 6:7-8: *"Do not be deceived: God cannot be mocked. A man reaps what he sows. Whoever sows to please their flesh, from the flesh will reap destruction; whoever sows to please the Spirit, from the Spirit will reap eternal life."* This passage underscores a universal principle: actions have repercussions. Just as a farmer plants seeds and later harvests crops based on what was sown, humans experience outcomes that correspond to their moral or immoral choices.

This metaphor emphasizes personal accountability. When individuals choose selfishness, greed, or sin ("sowing to please the flesh"), they often face negative consequences such as broken relationships, guilt, or spiritual emptiness. Conversely, when they act with kindness, integrity, and faithfulness ("sowing to please the Spirit"), they cultivate positive results like inner peace, stronger connections with others, and spiritual growth.

Divine Justice and Accountability

The Bible consistently teaches that God holds humanity accountable for its actions. Revelation 22:12 states: *"Look, I am coming soon! My reward is with me, and I will give to each person according to what they have done."* This verse highlights two key aspects of divine justice:

1. **Rewards for Righteousness:** Those who live according to God›s commandments and strive for goodness are promised rewards in this life and in eternity.

2. **Consequences for Sin:** Those who reject God›s ways and persist in wrongdoing face judgment and separation from Him.

This duality reflects God's fairness—He does not impose arbitrary punishments or blessings but rather allows individuals to experience the natural results of their choices.

Examples from Scripture

Throughout Scripture, there are numerous examples illustrating how choices lead to specific consequences:

1. **Adam and Eve (Genesis 3):** Their decision to disobey God by eating from the Tree of Knowledge resulted in expulsion from Eden, pain in childbirth for Eve, toil for Adam in cultivating food, and ultimately death entering the world.

2. **Cain›s Murder of Abel (Genesis 4): Cain›s jealousy led him to kill his brother Abel.** As a consequence, he was cursed by God to wander restlessly on Earth.

3. **David's Adultery with Bathsheba (2 Samuel 11-12):** King David›s sinful actions led to personal grief—the death of his child—and turmoil within his family.

4. **The Good Samaritan (Luke 10:25-37):** In contrast to these negative examples, this parable illustrates how choosing compassion over indifference leads to healing and restoration.

These stories demonstrate that while humans are free to make their own decisions, they are not free from the outcomes those decisions bring.

The Ripple Effect of Choices

Choices do not exist in isolation; they often have ripple effects that influence others beyond the individual making them. For example:

- A single act of kindness can inspire others to pay it

forward.

- Conversely, one person's dishonesty can erode trust within an entire community.

This interconnectedness underscores why moral responsibility extends beyond oneself—it impacts families, societies, and even future generations.

Grace Amid Consequences

While Scripture emphasizes accountability for one's actions, it also offers hope through God's grace. Even when individuals make poor choices leading to negative consequences, repentance can bring forgiveness and restoration (1 John 1:9). For instance:

- After denying Jesus three times (Luke 22:54-62), Peter repented deeply and was later restored by Christ (John 21:15-19).

- The Apostle Paul persecuted Christians before encountering Jesus on the road to Damascus (Acts 9). His transformation demonstrates how even grave sins can be redeemed through divine mercy.

God's grace does not erase all earthly consequences—for example, David still faced turmoil after his sin—but it provides spiritual renewal and a path toward reconciliation with Him.

Practical Implications for Today

Understanding that choices carry consequences has profound implications for daily living:

1. **Moral Responsibility:** Recognizing that every action has an outcome encourages individuals to think carefully before acting impulsively or selfishly.

2. **Long-Term Perspective:** Instead of seeking immediate gratification («sowing to please the flesh»), people are inspired to consider how their decisions align with eternal values («sowing to please the Spirit»).

3. **Encouragement Toward Goodness:** Knowing that righteous actions yield positive results motivates believers toward love, generosity, honesty, and other virtues.

In modern contexts—whether navigating relationships at home or ethical dilemmas at work—the principle remains timeless: wise choices lead toward flourishing; unwise ones lead toward hardship.

Conclusion

The relationship between free will and consequences is central both biblically and practically. Galatians 6:7 reminds us that our actions matter deeply—they shape our character now while influencing our eternal destiny later on (Revelation 22:12). By understanding this truth fully—and relying on

God's grace when we fall short—we can strive daily toward lives marked by goodness rather than regretful missteps into evil paths.

Chapter 9: Redemption Through Christ's Sacrifice

The concept of redemption through Jesus Christ is central to Christian theology and serves as the cornerstone for understanding how humanity can be reconciled with God despite the misuse of free will. This chapter explores the profound role that Jesus' sacrifice plays in addressing the consequences of human sin, which arises from the exercise of free will, and highlights key biblical passages such as John 3:16 and Acts 4:27–28.

The Problem of Sin and Free Will

From a theological perspective, sin entered the world through humanity's misuse of free will. In Genesis 3, Adam and Eve exercised their God-given ability to choose by disobeying His command not to eat from the Tree of Knowledge of Good and Evil. This act introduced sin into the world, creating a separation between humanity and God. The Apostle Paul explains this in Romans 5:12: "Therefore, just as sin entered the world through one man, and death through sin, in this way death spread to all people because all sinned."

Sin is often described as any action or thought that goes against God's will or law (1 John 3:4). It is a direct consequence of free will because it requires an individual to make a conscious choice to deviate from righteousness. While free will allows humans to love and obey God voluntarily, it also opens the door for rebellion against Him.

The problem lies in humanity's inability to fully overcome sin on its own. As Paul writes in Romans 3:23, "For all have sinned and fall short of the glory of God." Sin carries with it both spiritual and eternal consequences—separation from God (Isaiah 59:2) and ultimately death (Romans 6:23). Without divine intervention, humanity would remain trapped in this state.

The Necessity of Redemption

Redemption refers to the act of being saved or delivered from sin's power and its consequences. In Christian theology, redemption is made possible only through Jesus Christ's atoning sacrifice on the cross. This sacrificial act addresses both the justice and mercy of God.

God's justice demands that sin be punished because He is holy and cannot tolerate unrighteousness (Habakkuk 1:13). However, His mercy provides a way for sinners to be forgiven without compromising His justice. This balance is achieved through Jesus Christ, who took upon Himself the punishment for humanity's sins.

John 3:16 encapsulates this truth succinctly: "For God so loved the world that He gave His one and only Son, that whoever believes in Him shall not perish but have eternal life." This verse highlights God's immense love for humanity—a love so great that He was willing to send His Son to die on behalf of sinners.

The Role of Jesus Christ

Jesus Christ plays a unique role in redemption because He is both fully divine and fully human (John 1:14; Colossians 2:9). As a sinless human being (Hebrews 4:15), He was able to serve as a perfect substitute for sinful humanity. At the same time, His divinity ensured that His sacrifice had infinite value, sufficient to atone for all sins.

The Gospels describe how Jesus willingly laid down His life on the cross (John 10:18), enduring physical suffering and spiritual separation from God as He bore the weight of humanity's sins (Matthew 27:46). This act fulfilled Old Testament prophecies about a suffering servant who would bear the sins of many (Isaiah 53).

Acts 4:27–28 provides further insight into God's sovereignty over these events. It states: "Indeed Herod and Pontius Pilate met together with the Gentiles and the people of Israel in this city to conspire against your holy servant Jesus, whom you anointed. They did what your power and will had decided beforehand should happen." These verses affirm that Jesus' crucifixion was not an accident but part of God's predetermined plan for redemption.

The Implications for Humanity

Through His death on the cross, Jesus paid the penalty for sin once and for all (Hebrews 10:10). This means that anyone who places their faith in Him can receive forgiveness and be reconciled with God (Ephesians 2:8–9). Paul explains this beautifully in Romans 5:8–9: "But God proves His own love for us in that while we were still sinners, Christ died for us! How much more then, since we have now been justified by His blood, will we be saved through Him from wrath."

Redemption also brings freedom from sin's power. While believers still struggle with temptation due to their fallen nature (Romans 7), they are no longer enslaved by it because they have been given new life through Christ (2 Corinthians 5:17). The Holy Spirit empowers them to live righteously by transforming their hearts and minds (Galatians 5:16–25).

Finally, redemption offers hope for eternal life—a future where believers will dwell with God forever in a restored creation free from pain or suffering (Revelation 21:1–4).

Conclusion

Jesus Christ's sacrifice on the cross stands as God's ultimate solution to humanity's misuse of free will. By taking upon Himself the punishment deserved by sinners, He made it possible for them to be forgiven, transformed, and reconciled with their Creator. As John writes in his Gospel account, "Whoever believes in Him is not condemned" (John 3:18).

This profound truth underscores both God's justice—sin must be punished—and His mercy—He provided a way out through Jesus Christ. For Christians today, redemption serves as both a source of gratitude toward God's grace and motivation to live lives that honor Him.

Chapter 10: The Eschatological Restoration of Free Will

The concept of eschatology, or the study of the "end times," is a central theme in Christian theology. It encompasses the ultimate fulfillment of God's plan for humanity and creation, including the restoration of all things to their intended state. One fascinating aspect of eschatology is how it addresses the future of human free will. This chapter explores the idea that in the eschaton—the final culmination of history—humans will retain their free will but will no longer be subject to evil influences. This notion is deeply rooted in biblical texts, particularly Revelation 21, which describes a new heaven and a new earth where sin, suffering, and death are eradicated.

The Nature of Free Will in Christian Theology

Free will is one of the most profound gifts given by God to humanity. It allows individuals to make moral choices and distinguishes humans from other creatures. However, free will also comes with significant responsibility because it enables both good and evil actions. Throughout history, this dual potential has been evident in human behavior, as people have used their agency for acts of love and kindness as well as for sin and destruction.

In Christian theology, free will is not merely about choosing between good and evil; it is also about choosing to align oneself with God's will. This alignment becomes increasingly important when considering the eschatological promises found in Scripture.

The Promise of a New Creation

Revelation 21:1-4 provides a vivid description of what theologians often refer to as the "new creation." In this passage, John writes:

"Then I saw 'a new heaven and a new earth,' for the first heaven and the first earth had passed away, and there was no longer any sea. I saw the Holy City, the new Jerusalem, coming down out of heaven from God, prepared as a bride beautifully dressed for her husband. And I heard a loud voice from the throne saying, 'Look! God's dwelling place is now among the people, and he will dwell with them. They will be his people, and God himself will be with them and be their God. He will wipe every tear from their eyes. There will be no more death' or mourning or crying or pain, for the old order of things has passed away."

This vision portrays a world where suffering has ceased to exist—a stark contrast to our current reality where evil often seems pervasive. Importantly, while Revelation does not explicitly mention free will in this context, it implies that humanity's relationship with God will be fully restored without coercion or compulsion.

Freedom Without Evil Influences

One key question arises when considering free will in an eschatological framework: How can humans retain free agency if there is no longer any presence of evil? To answer this question, it is essential to understand that freedom does not necessarily require opposition between good and evil; rather, true freedom exists when individuals are liberated from sin's corrupting influence.

In Romans 8:21-23, Paul speaks about creation being set free from its "bondage to decay" into "the glorious freedom of the children of God." This passage suggests that freedom in its fullest sense involves liberation from all forms of corruption—not just external temptations but also internal inclinations toward sin.

Theologians like Augustine have argued that true freedom comes not from having equal access to good and evil but from being wholly aligned with goodness itself. In his work *City of God*, Augustine describes how those who are redeemed by Christ experience a transformation that enables them to choose good freely without being tempted by evil.[1] In this view, eschatological freedom involves perfect harmony between human desires and divine purposes.

The Defeat of Evil

Another critical aspect of eschatology is the complete defeat of Satan and all forces opposed to God's kingdom. Revelation 20:10 describes Satan being thrown into the lake of fire—a symbolic representation of his ultimate destruction:

"And the devil who deceived them was thrown into the lake of burning sulfur... They will be tormented day and night forever and ever."

With Satan defeated once and for all, his ability to tempt

humanity ceases entirely. Similarly, Revelation 21:27 states that nothing impure or deceitful can enter God's holy city:

"Nothing impure will ever enter it... but only those whose names are written in the Lamb's book of life."

These passages affirm that in God's restored creation there will be no external sources capable of leading humans astray.

Retaining Free Will in Eternity

While Scripture assures us that evil will be eradicated in eternity (Revelation 21:4), it does not suggest that humans lose their capacity for choice. Instead, redeemed individuals are depicted as willingly worshiping God (Revelation 7:9-12). Their worship arises not out of obligation but out of genuine love and gratitude for God's grace.

This voluntary devotion reflects what theologians call "confirmed righteousness"—a state where individuals freely choose righteousness because they have been transformed by God's sanctifying power.[2] In this state:

1. Humans retain their ability to make choices.

2. Their choices are always aligned with God's perfect goodness.

3. They experience true joy because they are no longer burdened by sin or its consequences.

Implications for Humanity's Future

The eschatological restoration described in Revelation offers profound hope for believers today. It assures us that while we currently struggle against sin and temptation (Ephesians 6:12), these challenges are temporary. In eternity:

- Our relationship with God will be fully restored.

- We will enjoy perfect communion with Him without fear or shame.

- Our capacity for love—both toward God and others—will reach its fullest potential.

This vision underscores why free will remains central even within an eternal context: It allows us not only to reflect God's image but also to participate actively in His redemptive plan throughout eternity.

In conclusion, the eschatological restoration described in Revelation presents a future where humans retain their free agency while being liberated from all forms of evil influence—a state characterized by perfect harmony between human desires and divine purposes.

Chapter 11: Misconceptions About Free Will and Predestination

The concepts of free will and predestination have been subjects of theological debate for centuries, often leading to confusion and misunderstanding. This chapter seeks to clarify these ideas by addressing common misconceptions and examining how they coexist within the framework of Christian theology. Using biblical examples, such as the narrative in 1 Samuel 23:1-14, we will explore how God's foreknowledge does not negate human free will.

Understanding Predestination and Foreknowledge

Predestination is often misunderstood as the idea that God has predetermined every action and decision of every individual, leaving no room for personal choice or agency. This interpretation can lead to a fatalistic worldview where human effort and moral responsibility are seen as irrelevant. However, a closer examination of scripture reveals a more nuanced understanding.

In Christian theology, predestination refers to God's sovereign plan for salvation. Passages like Romans 8:29-30 state that those whom God "foreknew" He also "predestined" to be conformed to the image of His Son. This does not imply that God forces individuals into specific choices but rather that He has a divine plan for humanity's redemption. Foreknowledge, on the other hand, means that God knows all things—past, present, and future—but this knowledge does not interfere with human free will.

The Example of 1 Samuel 23:1-14

A compelling biblical example that illustrates the distinction between foreknowledge and predestination is found in 1 Samuel 23:1-14. In this passage, David learns that the Philistines are attacking Keilah, a city in Judah. David seeks guidance from God through prayer, asking whether he should go to Keilah to save it. God responds affirmatively, assuring David that He will deliver the Philistines into his hands.

After defeating the Philistines and saving Keilah, David learns that King Saul is plotting to capture him there. Once again, David consults God through prayer, asking two specific questions: (1) Will Saul come down to Keilah? (2) Will the people of Keilah surrender him to Saul? God answers both questions affirmatively—Saul will come down, and the people of Keilah will betray David.

Armed with this knowledge, David chooses to leave Keilah with his men before Saul arrives. As a result, Saul abandons his pursuit of David at Keilah.

This story demonstrates several key points about foreknowledge and free will:

1. **God's Foreknowledge Does Not Dictate Human**

Actions

In this narrative, God reveals what *would* happen if certain conditions were met—namely, if David stayed in Keilah. However, David's decision to leave changes the outcome entirely. This shows that while God knows all possible outcomes based on human choices, His knowledge does not force those choices or outcomes into being.

2. **Human Free Will Operates Within Divine Sovereignty**

   Although God knew what would happen if David remained in Keilah, He did not compel David to stay or leave; the decision was entirely David's own. This illustrates how human free will operates within the broader scope of God's sovereignty.

3. **Foreknowledge Includes Contingent Events**

   The fact that God could predict what would happen under specific circumstances highlights His omniscience—not only does He know what *will* happen but also what *could* happen under different scenarios.

Common Misconceptions Addressed

Misconception #1: Foreknowledge Equals Causation

One common misunderstanding is the belief that if God knows an event will occur, He must have caused it to happen. The story of David at Keilah refutes this notion by showing that God's foreknowledge includes contingent possibilities based on human decisions.

For example:

- If David had stayed in Keilah, Saul would have come down.

- If David left (as he did), Saul would not pursue him there. God's knowledge encompasses all potential outcomes without forcing any particular one into existence.

Misconception #2: Predestination Eliminates Free Will

Another misconception is that predestination implies humans have no real choice because their actions are predetermined by God's plan. However, as seen in Romans 8:29-30 and Ephesians 1:4-5, predestination primarily concerns God's overarching plan for salvation rather than micromanaging individual decisions.

In practical terms:

- Predestination ensures that God's purpose for humanity—redemption through Christ—is fulfilled.

- It does not mean every individual action or choice is preordained without personal agency.

Misconception #3: Free Will Contradicts Divine Sovereignty

Some argue that if humans have true free will, it undermines God's sovereignty over creation. However, scripture consistently portrays a harmonious relationship between divine sovereignty and human freedom:

- Proverbs 16:9 states: "The heart of man plans his way, but the Lord establishes his steps."

- Philippians 2:12-13 encourages believers to "work out your own salvation with fear and trembling," while acknowledging "it is God who works in you."

These verses illustrate how human effort and divine guidance coexist without contradiction.

Reconciling Free Will and Predestination

The tension between free will and predestination can be resolved by understanding their complementary roles in Christian theology:

- **Free Will:** Humans are moral agents capable of making meaningful choices.

- **Predestination:** God›s sovereign plan ensures ultimate outcomes align with His purposes without negating individual freedom. This balance reflects both God›s omnipotence and His respect for human agency—a theme echoed throughout scripture.

Conclusion

The relationship between free will and predestination is complex but not contradictory when viewed through a biblical lens. As demonstrated in 1 Samuel 23:1-14:

- God's foreknowledge includes all possible outcomes based on human decisions.

- Human free will operates within divine sovereignty without negating either principle. By addressing these misconceptions head-on using scriptural examples like David at Keilah—and passages from Romans or Ephesians—we gain deeper insight into how these doctrines work together harmoniously within Christian faith.

Chapter 12: Living with Free Will Today: Practical Applications

Free will is a gift that allows individuals to make choices that shape their lives and influence the world around them. However, living with free will in a world filled with moral challenges and temptations requires intentional effort, discipline, and reliance on spiritual guidance. This chapter provides practical advice for navigating daily life while exercising free will responsibly and making righteous decisions.

Understanding the Importance of Daily Choices

Every day presents countless opportunities to exercise free will, from small decisions like how we spend our time to larger moral dilemmas that test our character. Scripture emphasizes the importance of being vigilant in our choices. For example, Matthew 26:41 states, "Watch and pray so that you will not fall into temptation. The spirit is willing, but the flesh is weak." This verse highlights the need for constant awareness and spiritual preparation to resist temptation.

Living with free will means recognizing that each choice carries consequences—both immediate and eternal. Galatians 6:7 reminds us, "Do not be deceived: God cannot be mocked. A man reaps what he sows." By understanding this principle, individuals can approach their decisions with greater responsibility and foresight.

Resisting Temptation Through Prayer

One of the most effective ways to resist temptation is through prayer. Prayer serves as a direct line of communication with God, providing strength, guidance, and clarity in moments of uncertainty or weakness. Jesus Himself modeled this practice when He prayed in the Garden of Gethsemane before His crucifixion (Matthew 26:36-44). His example demonstrates the power of prayer in aligning one's will with God's purpose.

Incorporating prayer into daily routines can help individuals stay grounded and focused on making righteous choices. Whether it's starting the day with a morning prayer for guidance or pausing during moments of stress to seek divine assistance, consistent communication with God strengthens resolve against temptation.

The Role of Scripture Study

Another essential tool for living righteously is regular scripture study. The Bible serves as a moral compass, offering wisdom and instruction for navigating life's challenges. Psalm 119:105 declares, "Your word is a lamp to my feet and a light to my path," illustrating how scripture illuminates the way forward in times of darkness or confusion.

By dedicating time each day to reading and reflecting on biblical teachings, individuals can internalize principles that guide their actions. For instance:

- Proverbs 3:5-6 advises believers to "Trust in the Lord with all your heart and lean not on your own understanding; in all your ways submit to Him, and He will make your paths straight."

- Ephesians 6:10-18 describes the "armor of God," encouraging Christians to equip themselves spiritually against evil influences.

Through consistent engagement with scripture, individuals develop a deeper understanding of God's expectations and are better equipped to make choices aligned with His will.

Building Accountability Through Community

Living righteously is not meant to be a solitary endeavor. Surrounding oneself with like-minded individuals who share similar values can provide encouragement, accountability, and support in making good choices. Hebrews 10:24-25 urges believers to "consider how we may spur one another on toward love and good deeds" while continuing to meet together for mutual edification.

Participating in faith-based communities—such as church groups or Bible studies—offers opportunities for fellowship and shared growth. These settings allow individuals to discuss challenges they face in exercising free will responsibly while learning from others' experiences.

Practicing Self-Control

Self-control is a critical aspect of living righteously with free will. Galatians 5:22-23 lists self-control as one of the fruits of the Spirit—a quality cultivated through spiritual maturity and reliance on God's strength. Developing self-control involves:

1. **Identifying Triggers:** Recognizing situations or behaviors that lead to poor decision-making.

2. **Setting Boundaries:** Establishing limits that prevent exposure to unnecessary temptations.

3. **Seeking Help When Needed:** Turning to trusted mentors or counselors for guidance during difficult times.

By practicing self-control consistently, individuals can overcome impulses that might otherwise lead them astray.

Conclusion

Living with free will today requires intentionality, discipline, and reliance on spiritual resources such as prayer, scripture study, community support, and self-control. While challenges are inevitable in a world filled with moral complexities, these practices empower individuals to make righteous choices that honor God's gift of free agency.

As Romans 12:2 encourages believers: "Do not conform to the pattern of this world but be transformed by the renewing of your mind." By committing daily efforts toward aligning one's actions with divine principles, it becomes possible not only to resist temptation but also to live a life marked by purpose, integrity, and faithfulness.

Conclusion: The Paradox of Free Will and Divine Sovereignty

The journey through this book has explored the profound theological interplay between free will and divine sovereignty. At its core, the question of whether humans truly have free will or whether everything is predestined by God remains one of the most debated topics in theology. While scripture provides evidence for both perspectives, reconciling these ideas requires a nuanced understanding of God's nature and His purpose for humanity.

Throughout the Bible, we see instances where God allows individuals to exercise their free will, making choices that lead to either righteousness or sin. For example, Adam and Eve's decision in the Garden of Eden was a clear demonstration of human agency (Genesis 3). However, there are also moments where scripture suggests that God intervenes directly in human decisions, such as when He "hardened Pharaoh's heart" during the Exodus narrative (Exodus 9:12). This duality raises important questions about how much control God exerts over human actions and whether our choices are truly our own.

The concept of God hardening hearts is particularly challenging to understand. In passages like Romans 9:18, Paul writes, "Therefore God has mercy on whom he wants to have mercy, and he hardens whom he wants to harden." This suggests that God's will is ultimately sovereign and that He can influence human decisions to fulfill His divine plan. Yet, this does not necessarily negate the existence of

free will; rather, it highlights the complexity of God's inter-
action with humanity. From a theological perspective, God's
hardening of hearts may serve a greater purpose—one that
aligns with His omniscient understanding of what is necessary for His ultimate plan for creation.

Predestination further complicates this discussion. Ephesians 1:4-5 states that God "chose us in Him before the
foundation of the world," implying that certain aspects of
our lives are predetermined by divine decree. However,
this does not mean that humans are mere puppets without
agency. Instead, many theologians argue that predestination operates within the framework of free will—God's foreknowledge allows Him to know our choices without forcing
them upon us (Romans 8:29-30). This perspective maintains that while God's plan is sovereign and unchangeable,
it still accommodates human freedom.

Ultimately, the coexistence of free will and predestination reflects a divine mystery that may be beyond full human comprehension. As finite beings attempting to understand an
infinite Creator, we must accept that some aspects of God's
nature and plan remain inscrutable. What we do know from
scripture is that God's intentions are always rooted in love
(1 John 4:8) and justice (Deuteronomy 32:4). Whether
through granting us agency or guiding events according to
His will, everything He does serves a higher purpose for
good (Romans 8:28).

For believers today, this paradox should not lead to despair
or confusion but rather inspire faith and trust in God's wis-

dom. While we may not fully grasp how free will and pre-destination coexist, we can take comfort in knowing that our lives are part of a larger divine narrative—a story authored by a loving Creator who desires our ultimate redemption.

In conclusion, whether viewed through the lens of free will or predestination—or perhaps both simultaneously—the relationship between humanity and God underscores one essential truth: we are called to live lives aligned with His purposes. By seeking righteousness in our choices while trusting in His sovereignty over all things, we fulfill our role as participants in His grand design. The tension between freedom and destiny invites us into deeper reflection on who God is and what it means to be created in His image—a mystery worth pondering for eternity.

Conclusion Prayer for Clarity and Understanding

Heavenly Father,
We come before You with humble hearts, seeking wisdom and understanding as we reflect on the truths shared in this book. Your Word reminds us that "now we see through a glass, darkly; but then face to face: now I know in part; but then shall I know even as also I am known" (1 Corinthians 13:12). Lord, we acknowledge that there are mysteries of Your divine plan that are beyond our comprehension, yet we trust in Your perfect will and infinite wisdom.

Father, we recognize that You are sovereign over all creation. In Your providence, You have allowed us the gift of free will while working all things according to the counsel of Your will (Ephesians 1:11). We do not always understand why hearts are hardened or why certain paths are predestined, but we trust that Your purposes are good and just. Help us to rest in the assurance that "all things work together for good to them that love God, to them who are the called according to His purpose" (Romans 8:28).

Lord, grant clarity to every reader of this book. Open their minds and hearts to discern the truths about free will, choice, and Your divine sovereignty. May they find peace in knowing that You have given us the ability to choose righteousness while providing grace through Jesus Christ when we fall short. Strengthen their faith as they navigate life's challenges and temptations, always remembering that You are with them every step of the way.

We pray for humility as we grapple with these profound concepts. Let us not lean on our own understanding but instead trust in You with all our hearts (Proverbs 3:5-6). May this book inspire deeper reflection on Your Word and a closer relationship with You.

Finally, Lord, may each reader be filled with hope and joy in knowing that one day all questions will be answered when we stand before You face to face. Until then, guide us by Your Spirit so that our choices glorify You and align with Your eternal purposes.

In Jesus' name,
Amen.

He who rebukes a man will later find more favor

than one who flatters with his tongue.

He who trusts in himself is a fool,

but one who walks in wisdom will be safe.

A faithful man will abound with blessings,

but one eager to be rich will not go unpunished.

Whoever turns his ear away from hearing the law,

even his prayer is detestable.

Prayer for Lulu and Me: Feeding the Poor

Here's a prayer for you and Lulu, incorporating wisdom and guidance for your plan to feed the poor:

Heavenly Father, we come before you with grateful hearts, seeking your guidance and blessings as Lulu and I embark on this journey to feed the poor. We are inspired by your Word, which calls us to care for the needy and to act justly and love mercy [1]. We recognize that you have a special place in your heart for the poor and marginalized, and we desire to reflect your compassion in our actions.

Lord, we ask for your wisdom as we begin this endeavor. Grant us discernment in identifying those most in need and in determining the most effective ways to provide nourishment and support. Help us to be sensitive to their needs, both physical and emotional, and to approach them with humility and respect.

Guide us in managing our resources wisely, so that we may be good stewards of what you have entrusted to us. Give us the strength to overcome any obstacles or challenges that may arise, and to remain steadfast in our commitment to serving others.

We pray for your protection over this ministry, that it may be free from corruption and that it may bring glory to your name. May our actions be a testament to your love and grace, and may they inspire others to join us in this important work.

Lord, give us wisdom, as Lulu and I begin to feed the poor.

We ask all this in the name of Jesus, who came to serve and to give his life for us. Amen.

Bless Lulu and me with patience, understanding, and a deep love for those we serve. Help us to see them as our brothers and sisters, created in your image, and to treat them with the dignity and respect they deserve

The kingdom of
heaven
is like
a merchant
in search of fine
pearls.

en he found one
very precious pearl,
he went away
and sold all he had
and bought it.

Those who forsake the law praise the wicked,

but those who keep the law resist them.

Evil men do not understand justice,

but those who seek the LORD comprehend fully.

Better a poor man who walks with integrity

than a rich man whose ways are perverse.

God Made Satan to Give Us Free Will to Choose

About Apostle Bill Amor

Apostle Bill Amor's life is a testament to the power of faith, perseverance, and divine intervention. Diagnosed with autism as a
child and considered high-functioning as an adult, Apostle Amor
has faced challenges that would have broken many. His journey
from despair to spiritual awakening forms the foundation of his
new book, Repent, which seeks to inspire readers to find hope and
redemption through God.

Born into a world that often misunderstood him, young Bill strug-
gled with feelings of isolation and inadequacy. Despite these challenges, he displayed remarkable determination. At the age of 12,
he achieved a significant milestone by winning a reading competi-
tion—an accomplishment that filled him with pride and optimism.
However, this joy was short-lived when his mother tearfully shared
devastating news from the doctor: he was not expected to live
beyond the age of 28 to 32.

This revelation shattered his world. Overwhelmed by fear and
hopelessness, Bill sought solace in his best friend John Straw, only
to discover that John had been taken away by his brother Andy.
Feeling abandoned and consumed by anger, he fled into the woods
near his home. It was there, amidst the trees and shadows of doubt,
that he cried out to God in desperation.

Bill's life changed forever on that fateful day. As he climbed a steep
hill toward his neighbor's house, he encountered what can only be
described as a divine vision: Jesus Christ Himself appeared before
him at the top of the hill near a chain-link fence. The image was
vivid—Jesus stood before him with pockmarks where His beard
had been removed and glistening divots on His cheeks and chin.
He did not resemble traditional depictions; instead, He appeared

timeless yet distinct from modern trends.

This miraculous encounter marked the beginning of Apostle Amor's transformation. From a young boy who felt lost and unworthy, he grew into a man devoted to spreading God's message of love and repentance. Through trials and tribulations—including struggles with literacy—he found strength in faith and discovered his purpose as an apostle.

Apostle Bill Amor shares his deeply personal story, as his journey serves as an inspiration for anyone grappling with doubt or seeking meaning in their lives.

Apostle Amor's mission is clear: to guide others toward spiritual healing by sharing his testimony of divine grace. With humility born from hardship and wisdom gained through faith, he invites readers to embark on their own journeys toward repentance and renewal.

www.ingramcontent.com/pod-product-compliance
Lightning Source LLC
Chambersburg PA
CBHW071338130626

46556CB00004B/1939

* 9 7 9 8 9 9 9 5 6 9 6 0 8 *